I dedicate Fun Smiles to the children
of our world. Within their smiles and sincere
laughter I find inspiration.

Keep smiling and sharing the inspirational joy
of laughter with others. Yours truly, King of Smiles.
Dwayne S. Henson

To order additional copies of this book, contact:
Xlibris
1-888-795-4274
www.Xlibris.com
Orders@Xlibris.com

Discover the inspirational magic created from
smiles through the guidance of Mr. Sunny Sunshine.

"Fun Smiles"
Written and illustrated
by
Dwayne S. Henson

Hello! Hello! It's Mr. Sunny Sunshine and I'm rolling through to share lots of fun smiles with you. So just follow along with me to see how fun smiles can be.

Smiles are fun and colorful as can be, sometimes I find it hard to pick and choose one just for having fun.

Smile

Smile

Smile

Smile

Smile

Smiles are fun red. It's lots of fun to exercise with a smile.

Smiles are fun blue. Hey! Look what I can do with two blue smiles tied together with an umbrella too.

Smiles are fun purple too. "Yahoo!"

Smiles are fun orange, green, and yellow too.

Smiles are fun big.

Smiles are fun to juggle and balance small.

Smiles are fun to arrange and hang in a picture frame on your wall.

Smiles are fun tied to my feet, how neat
I now have green smiles tied to my feet.

Smiles are fun to see when you look in the mirror, because they always look happy and familiar.

Smiles are fun to dress up. Well, how do I look with this smile, bowtie, and top hat?

Smiles are fun and neat even to use as a comfortable living room seat.

Smiles are fun in the wind.

Smile snowmobiles are lots of fun to drive through the snow.

Smiles are also fun to see in the spring when many things begin to grow.

Did you ever wonder how smiles grow? I think I know. If you add a sprinkle of love and lots of hugs, smiles are sure to spread and grow.

Well as you see, smiles are fun in so many ways, shapes, sizes and different colors, but most of all smiles are a lot more fun when I can share one with you. "That's" what I like to do for fun smiles.

It was certainly my pleasure to share "Fun Smiles" with you today. I look forward to sharing a lot more fun smiles with you on another day.

So long for now and enjoy your day.

Next a special offer and a preview of more up coming Mr. Sunny Sunshine™ books. ⟶

A special offer from
the author / illustrator of the
Mr. Sunny Sunshine books
Dwayne S. Henson

Here's my special offer.
Two preschool educational
books combined in one at
one regular sales price.

For more information on this special offer
and other Mr. Sunny Sunshine books
Contact Xlibris at: 1-888-795-4274
www.Xlibris.com/DwayneHenson

Dwayne S. Henson
Creator of Mr. Sunny Sunshine™

My gift that I would like to share with others is to inspire those who are in need of a smile and to educate others of the positive inspirational value that smiles provide in our society.

With Mr. Sunny Sunshine™ as my tool in this never ending educational smile-based journey, I aim to demonstrate how smiles can be utilized in so many positive encouraging ways such as to inspire, motivate, educate as well as to entertain. How Mr. Sunny Sunshine™ creates smiles and shares them with others, I truly believe, are some of the fascinating trademark dynamics of this inspiring smile making concept.

As you may come to discover there's more inspirational magic behind a smile than what we generally see.

From this unique unit of books you'll learn how and why Mr. Sunny Sunshine™ took it upon himself to create more smiles and inspiration all over the world. Along with this you'll also be provided with a one-of-a-kind, entertaining, smile-based education and much, much, more.

There's a lot to uncover and learn about a smile. I invite you to journey along to see how truly motivating a smile can be.

I certainly hope you enjoy my Mr. Sunny Sunshine™ books as much as I did creating them for others to share. I look forward to creating lots more smiles for many of years to come.

Sincerely, Dwayne S. Henson... Prince of happiness, King of smiles.

Printed in the United States
By Bookmasters